The
Little People's Pageant of
Cornish Legends

The
Little People's Pageant of
Cornish Legends

ERIC QUAYLE
MICHAEL FOREMAN

A Little Simon Book
Published by Simon & Schuster, Inc., New York

1 2 3 4 5 6 7 8 9 10
ISBN: 0-671-63580-8

Contents

For Benjamin Foreman and Eden Quayle

Introduction

In Germany the brothers Jacob and Wilhelm Grimm were busy collecting fairy and folk tales as early as 1806, later to be published as *Kinder und Hausmärchen* ("Nursery and Household Tales") in two volumes dated 1812 and 1814. No further attempt was made to collect the legends and folktales of any part of England, Scotland, or Wales until the appearance of *Popular Romances of the West of England,* 1865, which was issued in two volumes by the London publisher John Camden Hotten, with full-page illustrations by George Cruikshank. The editor and compiler was Robert Hunt (1807–87), who, although born just across the border in Devonport, spent most of his life in Cornwall.

Hunt was a scientist, a Fellow of the Royal Society, and a pioneer photographer, publishing his first book on the subject as early as 1841. Even as a boy, as he states in his preface to *Popular Romances of the West of England,* he was collecting on sheets of paper he had "stitched into the back of an old book" the tales and legends of Cornwall, "my purpose being to visit each relic of Old Cornwall, and to gather up every existing tale of its ancient people."

As far as he could discover, no legend or story had been written down, much less appeared in print, so it was by oral tradition, sitting in thatched cottages before hearths bright with burning furze, that young Hunt listened to the tales of grandmothers who remembered stories told to them by their own mothers and grandmothers way back in the eighteenth century.

It is from Robert Hunt's seminal work of 1865 that the plots of most of the stories you are about to read have been taken, embellished by the tales told to me by the present-day old folk of remote villages in West Penwith, the part of Cornwall that stretches from the Hayle River to Land's End. One other source was *Traditions and Hearthside Stories of West Cornwall,* 1870, 1873, 1880, by William Bottrell (1816–80), a three-volume work that complemented and added to Hunt's earlier collection.

One final pleasure I derived from retelling these legends of the Celtic past was the days spent visiting each of the sites and villages in the company of my friend Michael Foreman, an artist determined that his backgrounds should faithfully portray the primitive starkness of the granite outcrops and the ancient stone hedges built so laboriously by generations of Cornishmen way back in the mists of time. We watched, as they must have done, the speckled brown trout patrolling the pools in the Zennor River, overhung with the fuchsia lining its banks. When we reached the Mermaid's Seat, it was obvious that something wet had recently sat there. We looked at each other and waited in silence, but she did not appear. We decided that, when this book is published, we would leave a copy there.

ERIC QUAYLE

The Magic Ointment

Zennora Nankervis lived all alone in a cottage on the moors near Pendeen, supporting herself by selling or bartering her knitting, for which she was justly famous for many miles around. On a Saturday morning that dawned warm and sunny, she set out to walk the nine miles to Penzance. She badly needed a new pair of shoes and a fresh set of knitting needles, so counting out five of the King's shillings into her old leather purse she was soon on her way.

Zennora was a lonely old soul who always sought company, and by far her best friend was Hester Berryman, so she took the goats' path that led to the cliffs and the cottage of the woman whom the whole village knew to be a witch.

"Witch or no witch," said Zennora out loud, as she picked her way along the narrow path, "bad company is better than none."

And with that she stopped at Hester's rough wooden door and bent to peep through the keyhole. She could see Hester busily preparing a strange green ointment in a little pewter pot. Then her friend beckoned to the crouching hunchback figure of her son, who, for reasons best known to herself, she had named Quillet. As the misshapen creature limped toward her, Hester took a dab of ointment on the tip of her finger

13

and carefully rubbed both of Quillet's eyes with it. Then she put the pot of salve on the shelf by the chimney and covered it with her shawl.

Zennora knocked lightly on the door, lifted the latch, and went in so suddenly that both mother and son started and looked uneasy. Then Quillet muttered something and took his rough-spun cap from its peg and disappeared out across the moors. Hester so far recovered her composure as to say she was pleased to see her old friend and would she like a little drop of something to help her on her way?

"Sure, I'm off to Penzance," said Zennora, "and to cure the pain in me feet I'm for having a touch of brandy and rue, and you've the best in West Penwith."

So away went Hester into the other room for the bottle, and Zennora instantly lifted the edge of the shawl and dipped her finger in the pewter pot. She had only just enough time to touch her right eye with it before Hester returned with two old leather tankards and her bottle of brandy and rue.

Both of them swigged back the liquor in the leather cups, and it was then that Zennora suddenly realized that the house was swarming with little people. Some were swinging on cobwebs, others were playing pranks on the beams and rafters above her head, several were riding on mice and chasing each other in and out of the holes in the thatch. Zennora was amazed at the sight, but said nothing about the crowd of little imps to Hester. Feeling one of the little people light gently on her shoulder, she quickly handed back the tankard, said her good-byes, and started across the moors to Penzance. She looked back once and saw her tiny passenger scampering back to the cottage, up the granite wall, and into the thatch.

It was well past midday when she reached the town, which in those

days consisted almost entirely of Market Street and a few alleyways leading away from it. It was there the market was held, and Zennora was soon walking from stall to stall doing a little business here and there, selling some of her knitted garments and buying herself a fine pair of leather shoes. Then suddenly she saw Quillet limping his way between the stands, pausing now and then when something caught his eye before openly slipping it into the canvas bag he carried. Pewter spoons and plates, hanks of yarn, clay pipes, a leg of pork– all were lifted and inspected and then tucked into the bag. Yet Zennora was amazed to find that not a stall holder or any of those crowding around seemed to notice anything amiss. None of them seemed even to see Quillet or the bag he carried, though this was becoming heavier every minute.

Pushing her way through the crowd, Zennora watched for her opportunity, then suddenly took him by the arm so that he jumped as he turned to see her. "Quillet, Quillet! What do ye think you're about! Aren't thee ashamed to be carrying on sich a game? Your poor mother would die for the shame on't, that's for sure!"

The hunchback looked at first rather frightened. Then when he realized who was addressing him, his manner changed. "So it's you, Zennora." He peered intently at her face, then muttered a curse. "You old witch! Now tell me straight, which eye can ye see me with?"

"Which eye?"

"Aye, which eye?"

Zennora shut her left eye, and this made not a whit of difference, so she opened it and shut her right eye. Immediately Quillet disappeared, though all around him were the other folk just as before. When she opened her right eye again, there was the little hunchback grinning and grimacing at her, his bag slung over his hump and still heavy with the goods he had stolen. "Which eye, Zennora?" Zennora said nothing, but she felt very uneasy. "Come on, you old devil, right or left?"

"Don't ye talk to me like that!" She took a pace back. "But to be civil, I'll say 'tis strange, but there is something wrong with me left eye."

"Oh, then you see me with the right, do you!"

As he said this, Quillet moved toward her, thrusting out his finger, whose nail seemed like an adder's head. So fast did the hunchback strike

that he had touched her right eye before she had time to move her head. Instantly all went dark. From that moment, Zennora was stone blind in her right eye.

Though she could no longer see Quillet, she heard his ugly laughter as she stumbled away, bumping into stalls as she tried to find her bearings using her one good eye. How she found her way to the rab-covered* overpass and the road back to the treeless uplands above Pendeen she could never rightly remember. By that time she was so tired she could hardly drag one foot after the other, and had it not been for the stone walls bordering the lanes, she must surely have wandered off wherever her left eye took her. As it was, she twice tumbled into ditches on her blind side, emerging wet and bedraggled and crying with her one good eye. "If only," she said aloud, "if only I could find a quiet old horse to ride me 'ome."

* Rab is orange clay used to pave narrow lanes and farm tracks.

No sooner were the words out of her mouth than there at the roadside stood an old bony white horse, tangled up in its halter. Zennora fell on her knees with delight, untying the halter, which was looped around its front feet. Then she climbed unsteadily on top of the stone wall and swung her old legs over the horse's back, using the halter as makeshift reins. By this time the sun had set and the bats were flitting.

"Gee wup! Gee wup! K'up k'up, k'up!" and the rheumaticky old horse started a slow clip-clop across the moors, so slow in spite of Zennora's urging that she finally snatched a thorn stick from the hedge and brought it–thwack–with all her force across its tail. In an instant she felt herself flying through the air, the horse having completely disappeared like a burst balloon, and what she was gripping now was no longer its mane but a wooden broomstick.

"Take me to Hester Berryman's!" she shrieked, holding the stick and her bag of shopping as tight as tight. Gradually the broomstick altered course, and with her one good eye she saw the lights, first of Morvah village and then of Pendeen, and then, as they gradually dropped to what would have been treetop height if the gales had allowed any trees to grow on the windswept northern coast of Cornwall, Zennora sighted the thatch of Hester's cottage.

No sooner did her feet touch the ground than the broomstick stood itself upright and turned into a sea-loving tamarisk tree, its feathery branches shining with little pink and white flowers. As it happened on her blind side, Zennora saw nothing of this as she hurried to the door of the cottage to peep through the keyhole. There was no sign of Hester or of her hunchback son, but there was the shawl just as before. Quick as a flash Zennora was inside, hitting her head on a low beam because of her blind eye, then over to lift the shawl and dip her finger in the fairy salve. She rubbed her right eye with the ointment, keeping her left eye tightly closed. Sure enough she could see again, and the room was alive with the little Cornish sprites and spriggans as before. Then she rubbed some on her left eye, too, and as she did so she saw her image fade from the mirror on the wall and knew she was invisible to all but those anointed in similar fashion. How long the spell would last she had no idea, so to be on the safe side she pocketed the pewter pot and left the cottage to a chorus of squeaky good byes from the elves.

From that time onward she never saw Hester Berryman or Quillet again, though it was not long before the Cornish spriggans had found Zennora's cottage by following a thin thread of spider's web their leader had attached to the hem of her skirt. They arrived in twos and threes until the thatch was alive with their squeaks. They told her how to make more of the ointment by gathering four-leaf clovers at the full moon, and she showed them her thanks by knitting them fine jackets in Cornish tartan designs that were her own secret. She had plenty of time, for now there was no housework or gardening to do. The spriggans did all that. So Zennora took her ease and lived to be a hundred.

The Giants of St. Michael's Mount

Long, long ago there lived near the village of Marazion a Cornish giant and his wife. His name was Cormoran, and though he was the strongest giant in the land, he forced his wife Cormelian to do most of the work. At that time much of the land in Cornwall was thick forest, and Cormoran, despite his great strength, was always fearful that the Cornish peasants, whose land and cattle he constantly plundered, would one day creep up on him while he was asleep and kill both him and his wife.

He determined to build a hill high enough to let him see over the forest and beyond, with a castle to top it and windows to see through even when he was lying in his massive oaken bed. And just to make doubly sure, he would build his mount not on land but some way out to sea. No sooner had the idea come to him than he set Cormelian the task of gathering the largest granite boulders she could find. Then she was to put the rocks in her apron and carry them way out to sea so that first an island and then a mountain would rise up from the seabed.

Poor Cormelian worked day after day, lifting the huge granite rocks her husband pointed to with the tree he had shaped into a club, and only occasionally, when the rock he had selected proved too heavy even for the giantess to lift, did he stir himself to give his wife a pull and a heave.

Then off she tramped once more, striding with one pace over the wide shore, then into the sea, whatever the state of the tide, deeper and deeper to empty her apron of stones on the ever rising mount.

By late summer the pointed hill of granite could be seen for miles around, and Cormoran generously gave his wife a day of rest, as he called it, telling her to fetch and carry their furniture and household goods from the deep and gloomy cave they had dwelt in to the summit of the mount. Then he strode out to sea with his cudgel over his shoulder, sat down on the peak of his island, and prepared to conjure his castle from the air. Most giants can perform odd bits and pieces of magic, but for this event Cormoran had saved up his spells for many months, lumping their often tiny scraps of magic into one really big spell and using the entire energy to perform one massive bang. And a massive bang it was! From out of a clear blue sky came a clap of thunder that shook houses and cottages from Land's End to the Lizard, and then, as frightened villagers streamed out of their homes, there it was on top of the mount–a castle! A giant's castle, complete with pinnacles and turrets and narrow slitty windows that Cormoran could peer through and aim his slingshot at his enemies.

"Will the dreaded giant and his wife turn respectable and obey the laws of the land now that they have their own residence?" the villagers asked their elders. But almost before the words were out of their mouths, there came a roar from the direction of the mount and the thud of approaching footsteps that sent them fleeing to their homes. If anything, Cormoran seemed to require even more meat than ever, and he could be seen almost daily wading in two or three steps through the sea to stalk through the meadowland seeking the flocks of sheep and herds of cattle the good folk of Cornwall had reared and cared for. Once he had found them, he would pick up as many as three cows at a time, tying their tails together before throwing them over his shoulders while he stuffed sheep by the dozen into the sailcloth bag he carried.

The whole of West Penwith from St. Ives to Land's End was in despair, the villagers knowing they would face a winter of near starvation unless the giant could be killed. Frantically they gathered together all the gold they had hidden, and offered a leather bag heavy with coin to any man brave enough to undertake the task. But out of all the brave men of Cornwall only one young man volunteered. His name was Jack, and he lived with his father and mother in a cottage in the village of Ding Dong, high up on the moors. His parents begged him not to go, but Jack had made up his mind. Not only that—he had a plan!

That night Jack went to the seashore opposite the giants' castle and dug in the darkness for many hours until he had made a pit so deep that it was only by the rope ladder, whose end he had secured to a rock, that he was able to extricate himself. Next, he turned to the thin planks he had brought with him, carefully placing them over the pit to form a cover. Finally, he spread sand over the planks so that all looked just as usual. Then he sat himself down to wait.

The sun was high in the sky before Jack saw the massive door of the castle fly open and Cormoran emerge with his club as big as an oak. He gave his usual roar, which could be heard for miles around, but this time to his great surprise there came an answering shout, and there was young Jack jumping up and down on the far shore and waving his sword above his head. The giant could hardly believe his eyes. With a growl of rage he strode savagely across the channel of water, raising his massive club as he walked. Instead of running away, Jack stood still and even blew a blast on the horn he carried. This was too much for Cormoran, and he took a pace up the beach to squash this puny human with a single blow. As he did so, the ground gave way beneath his feet, and he fell into Jack's pit with only his ugly head sticking out. Quick as a flash, Jack ran behind him and, with a single blow of his sword, lopped off the giant's head.

From the cliffs above him he heard the sound of cheering, and looking back, he could see the grateful villagers dancing with joy. Suddenly they were silenced as from across the bay came a terrible scream. There was Cormelian, the giant's wife, advancing toward them. As he turned to flee, Jack noticed that she seemed smaller than usual, and as he gazed, she was visibly shrinking. Only magic had kept her and her husband so huge, and with his death the magic was waning and the spell getting weaker and weaker. She was only halfway across the water that separated the mount from the shore, and as she shrank, the sea came up to her waist, then to her shoulders until, with a final effort, she reached shallower waters. But she continued to shrink, first to smaller than human adult form, then to the size of a little girl. Then she was as small as a cat, then as tiny as a mouse. At that moment a sea gull swooped down, picked up the squeaking giantess, and flew off across Mount's Bay. No one ever saw her again.

The villagers once more emerged from behind the rocks where they had watched and waited, knowing nothing of the hidden pit and thinking that Jack was sure to die. Now, with both giants dead, their joy knew no bounds. The mayor of Penzance and the mayor of Marazion, and the mayor of St. Ives, all three came hurrying down the sands with the rest of the grateful Cornishmen to present the hero of the day with his well-earned bag of gold.

That night there were feasts and celebrations throughout all Cornwall, and at a special ceremony Jack was given a belt chased with silver on which was written:

> This is the valiant Cornishman
> Who slew the giant Cormoran.

Jack wore it wherever he went, and that's how he came to be called Jack the Giant-Killer!

Piggin

In the olden days, mothers in Cornwall, especially mothers whose babies were exceptionally pretty or handsome, were most careful to protect their infants from piskies discontented with their own small children. For it was the piskies' practice to steal small human babies from out of their cradles and substitute in their place their own ugly and bad-tempered offspring. The small people and the spriggans did not do this, and neither did the buccas or the brownies, their babies usually being quite pretty in a miniature sort of way. It was the Cornish piskies that all mothers in those days really feared!

Occasionally, little boys and little girls almost up to five years old suffered the same fate, though not nearly so often as babies in arms. However, it was wise to be careful, especially in the far west of Cornwall– West Penwith, as it was called– for there the piskies had their little villages and towns, always underground or under the waters of a lake or a spring or a pool.

One day, a long time ago, a young woman named Janey Tregeer lived in a thatched cottage at Brea Vean. It being a fine September day she decided to go out into the stone-walled field to reap the hay, leaving her baby in its cradle fast asleep. Before latching the door behind her, she

29

carefully covered the fire with damp peat, scattered the hot coals beneath the baking oven, and swept up the ashes on the hearthstone. Having made all safe, she had a last look at her pretty little baby, bent down and kissed its forehead, and then, taking her reaping hook from its nail, set out for the hay field. All that afternoon she worked away happily, helped by her two older children, who had been there with their father since first light. It was late in the afternoon when Janey returned to her cottage, and you may imagine her distress when the first thing she saw was the baby's overturned cradle, with the fine straw the child had been lying in so warmly, strewn all over the floor.

Where, oh, where was her baby? Frantically she searched the two rooms that were all the cottage boasted, but there was no sign of the child. With dusk already falling, she rushed back to the field where her two young sons and her husband were stacking the last piles of hay. Janey shouted the news to the startled trio. Dropping their tools, they ran back to the cottage, the father's hand trembling as he tried to light the lamp, his wife stirring the fire into flames to give more light. It was at that moment that all of them heard a sound between a cry and a moan, an unearthly guttural wail that made their blood run cold. It seemed to come from the large bundle of dried fern fronds that composed the two bigger boys' bed, but it was several seconds before the father slowly walked toward it.

No sooner had Willi Tregeer reached the mound of ferns than something stirred deep in the dried fronds so that he took a step backward. Then out of the middle of the heap a baby's head suddenly appeared, a little wizened face as ugly as a walnut, yet bearing some resemblance to their own sweet child. It opened its mouth to show a row of sharp pointed teeth, then once again emitted the chilling wail they had heard before.

"It be a changeling, Willi! It be a changeling!"

There was no doubting the fact, for every piskie baby has a full set of very sharp teeth from birth, and this specimen was showing his spiky mouthful every time he wailed.

"May the good Lord 'ave mercy on us!"

The farmer and his wife turned sorrowfully away, taking their young

30

sons' hands as they sat together in the far corner of the room. Occasionally one or the other of them would glance back to the fern bed in the hope that all this was just a delusion, but there was the white little face staring at them and seeming to grimace if they looked too long. Then the wailing started again.

"Devil take it back to 'ell!"

"I'll 'ave to feed um, Willi."

All of them knew that to harm or starve or try to kill the infant piskie would bring exactly the same fate to their own baby son. They had to be kind and caring to the changeling if they wanted the piskies to be benign and charitable to their little boy, so Janey forced herself to pick it up, shuddering slightly as she did so. It was wrapped in a garment made entirely of leaves from the dock weed, for the one thing no piskie is proof against is the sting of a nettle. They feel the pain far more than humans do, and no piskie would ever venture out without its own small piece of dock leaf to apply instantly to the skin if he gets stung. For a piskie baby to be stung meant almost certain death, so all their early clothes were made of dock leaves stitched together.

From that time onward the baby piskie was fed and watered (piskies don't drink milk), and as the months and years went by, it grew to its full height of about twelve inches. By that time its ears had assumed the sharply pointed shape of its race, as had its pointed nose. Willi and Janey tried to treat it as one of the family, remembering their own missing little boy, but there was no way in which they could deceive themselves into liking or loving the miniature intruder. The two elder boys always called it Piggin, and the name stuck. "What's Piggin up to?" or "Where's that drattin' Piggin?" became commonplace expressions, and there were times when either parent would gladly have smothered the ugly little changeling or secretly dropped it down the well.

There was a tradition in Cornwall at that time that if you beat a changeling with a broom made from the branches of a furze bush, until the child was black and blue all over, its real mother would come hurrying back with the human baby she had stolen. This was supposed to be to save her own piskie child from any further punishment, for piskies presumably loved their children as we do. The reason they swapped their offspring for a human child was that the piskie mother believed her baby was ailing and would better survive under human care– but she always made sure that the baby she stole was as pretty as her own was ugly. Now, Janey knew quite well the tradition about the beating, but despite the fact that the imp was invariably naughty and mischievous, she just could not bring herself to inflict a punishment so severe. At times her patience gave way to real anger, especially when the changeling got out of its shoebox bed in the middle of the night and started dancing around, beating a pewter plate with a spoon or deliberately creeping up to their bed and suddenly squealing in their ears. But each time they cuffed it across its head they seemed to hear their own

baby cry out, its voice mingling with the changeling's wails, so that Janey shed tears of frustration mixed with tears of pity for her own little boy, wherever he might be.

Thus it was that nearly three years went by, the Tregeer cottage being isolated and both the boys being pledged to secrecy, so that few if any of the occasional callers suspected that anything was wrong. If anyone was seen trudging across the fields to the cottage, Piggin was locked securely in a wooden box lined with wool and with only one little airhole for him to breathe through. Shout as much as he liked, the wool muffled the sound until the caller took his or her leave. Until one day they were surprised! None of the family had seen or heard the wrinkled old woman approaching until her head suddenly appeared at the open window as Piggin danced on the kitchen table, juggling a couple of knives. Quick as a flash, Janey snatched him up, thrust him into his wooden box, and locked it in her old oak chest in the far corner of the room. Then she turned to open the cottage door.

"What do you want, Grannie?"

The old woman was bent and frail, with a tattered hood pulled over her thin gray hair. In one hand she held a gnarled and twisted walking stick while on her other arm there rested the handle of a large wicker basket. Janey could see almost nothing of her face, but was conscious of a pair of piercing coal-black eyes that seemed to burn their way right into her mind. The old crone stretched out her hand and laid it on Janey's arm.

"Spare a bite an' a mug o' tay for a crittur that's worn with fastin' this whole day through."

Janey hesitated. Willi was away up the fields with their eldest son, while John, the younger boy, was in bed with measles.

"There's sickness in the house. My boy 'as the red rash."

The old woman crackled with laughter. "Then it's me that's 'ere to 'elp um, me 'ansom!"

Pushing open the door, she entered the cottage and went straight to the fern bed where the boy lay. The lad shrank away, but she took his hand in hers and held it tight. He had started to cry as she approached him, but now he stopped and called out to his mother: "She's warmin' me, Mum!"

The boy could feel a glow throughout his body, and when the witch let go of his hand and his mother came to the bed, she could see immediately that the rash had left him.

"She's laid 'er 'ands on you. You're better!"

The old woman gave another of her peculiar laughs and sat herself down on the three-legged milking stool while Janey busied herself preparing food. As she handed the old woman a mug of tea, she gave her thanks for the lad's recovery, for the boy was out of bed and dressed and away to the fields just as though he had never been ill.

"You're a witch, then, and no offense," said Janey as the woman munched her crusty home-baked bread, well spread with farmhouse butter.

"What if I do be?"

"No offense, mind!"

The witch finished her meal, wiping her mouth with the back of her hand, her wicker basket at her feet. Then she hobbled over to the oak chest and poked it with her stick. She turned to Janey, her toothless mouth creased in a wrinkled smile.

"Will you swap what's in 'ere for what's in there?" And she pointed with her stick to the wicker basket.

She had seen, then, thought Janey. She'd seen Piggin, sure enough! "You know, then?"

The witch nodded her head, asking the question again. "Come, now! Will you swap what's in 'ere for what's in there?"

A sudden glow of hope swept over Janey as she saw the wicker basket move a little. Could it be...?

"Yes, yes, yes, yes!" she shouted out the words, at the same time flinging open the chest and thrusting the box with the changeling inside into the old woman's hands. Then like a flash she was across the room and pulling at the basket's cover.

"My boy! My boy! My boy's back!" And she hugged her little boy to her, kissing his face and hair and laughing with happiness.

She turned to thank the old witch, but the room was empty. From that day onward the family prospered; all three boys grew to manhood, and the piskies troubled them no more. But the youngest son never spoke of what he had seen and done in the village underground. His mother noticed that he never drank milk and that he always carrried a dock leaf in his pocket– habits he had picked up elsewhere.

The Good Dog Devil

Long, long ago, in the days of the Cornish giants, a brave young miner from Morvah went out in the world in search of adventure. With a pack on his back and a stout thorn stick in his hand, he traveled many miles across the windswept moors that separate the Atlantic from the British Channel, as it was then called, but he met not a soul, though he journeyed for many hours.

At length, as evening closed the eyes of the world, he found himself on a wild and lonely mountain side, deserted by all but a small herd of thin and emaciated goats seeking what little food there was between the boulders of granite. He looked down toward the distant ocean, but there was not a village in sight, not even a lonely cottage whose lighted windows might have welcomed him. He had been following a faint and much overgrown path the goats used, but as darkness closed in, even that guide was lost. In vain he tried to find his way to any refuge, but the huge rocks and boulders seemed to hem him in on all sides. Faint and weary, he stumbled on in the darkness, and then suddenly, in a small and level clearing, he discerned a stone structure, a strange and eerie-looking structure of carefully placed rocks surmounted by a massive slab of granite that served as roof. As a boy he had been taken by his father to

37

see similar but far smaller piles such as this, and he knew it to be an ancient quoit, or burial chamber. "It be a quoit," he muttered, crossing himself as he crouched with his back to the keen east wind that seemed to search out each gap in his homespun clothes. Weary and cold as he was, he hesitated long before he plucked up enough courage to venture over to the entrance. It was pitch dark inside, with a smell of earth and rotting leaves, but the rain now falling on his back decided a very tired Harvey Trembath, and he crept silently inside. Here at least was shelter from the wind and rain, and he felt in his pack for the meat pie his mother had baked the day before and for the leather bottle containing the strong cold tea. He ate ravenously every crumb, then wiped his mouth with the back of his hand, wrapped his cloak around him, and lay down to fall almost instantly asleep.

He slept like a dead man for several hours, to suddenly jerk awake as a dreadful series of piercing screams froze the blood in his veins. For seconds he imagined it to be a dream, but the noise continued, the air resounding with the most terrible shrieks and yells. Despite his shaking hands and chattering teeth, the young Cornishman raised himself with his stick and in fear and trembling felt his way to where a sliver of moonlight shone through a gap in the wall.

The sight that met his eyes made him shrink back from the opening, but not before he had printed on his memory the awful scene that was to

haunt him for many a night. A troop of hideously large cats were engaged in a wild and frenzied dance, each upon its hind legs and all circling a huge black monster of an animal that waved its paws in time with the shrieks. Mingled with their unearthly cries young Harvey Trembath could clearly distinguish the words:

> "Don't let the devil know!
> Keep it close and dark!
> Don't let the devil know!
> We'll know him by his bark!"

The four lines were repeated over and over again in a high-pitched Cornish wail. The full moon shed its light on the gruesome scene which, despite himself, the young Cornishman felt compelled to watch again and again as the dance continued with unabated intensity.

Suddenly, the midnight hour being passed, the dancing stopped. The phantom cats, still upright, bowed once toward their leader. As a black cloud smothered the moon Harvey could see only shadows. Then as the light flooded back, a skein of steeple-hatted witches broomsticked their way across the valley below and were lost to sight behind Trewey Hill.

Despite the horror of what he had seen, Harvey fell back into sleep, and the sun was already high in the sky when at last he awoke. He could hardly believe he had witnessed such a scene, and pausing only to wash his face and hands in the pool beneath a spring bubbling from a cleft in the rocks below the burial chamber, he hurried down the mountainside. By the bright morning light he discovered a path he had missed the night before and hurried on. To his great joy he saw a scattered cottage or two and, beyond them, clustered around a squat-towered church, a small village.

Urged on by hunger, he had reached the village square when he heard the sound of a woman's voice raised loud in lamentation and entreaty. He stopped and called to her through the open cottage door. Other doors opened, and he was soon the center of a crowd of rustic villagers, all of whom looked sad and woebegone. Twice he asked if he could help them in any way, but all shook their heads, and many turned away. A woman pressed some bread and a can of milk into his hands as an old man shuffled forward and drew him aside. "Every year," he said, "the mountain spirit claims a victim. The time 'as come again, and this very night 'e will devour the prettiest bal-maiden* the village can produce. Now you know the cause of the wailing of 'er mother and of our own lamentation."

When the young Cornishman, filled with anger and resentment, turned from his bread and milk and asked why they let this happen, several others answered, saying that at sunset the young victim would be put into a wooden cage and carried up to the burial place where Harvey had spent the night. There she would be left alone. In the morning, when the bravest among them ventured up to the chamber, they would find that she had vanished, never to be seen again. So it was each year, and so it would be now. There was no help for it, and there was nothing he or anyone else could do to prevent it.

As he listened, Harvey Trembath determined to save the girl. He remembered the words of the cats' song:

> Don't let the devil know!
> Keep it close and dark!
> Don't let the devil know!
> We'll know him by his bark!

*Bal-maidens were unmarried young women who worked on the surface at tin and copper mines.

Bark? Did the devil bark? Harvey wondered. It was at that moment that a magnificent German shepherd dog walked majestically across the village square, king of the village dogs and proud of his domain. "What's his name?" Harvey asked.

"'Im? The old devil 'e is, and the devil we calls 'im!"

The young Cornishman did not stop to ask more questions, but hurried off to Devil's owner to beg him to lend him the dog for just one night. At first the farmer was unwilling, but at length he agreed to lend Devil after Harvey promised to bring him back personally the very next day. Overjoyed and feeling that his plan might work, Harvey hastened to the cottage of the unhappy maiden and begged her parents to keep her safely under lock and key until he returned and under no circumstances to let her out of their sight.

Four of the strongest young men of the village he told of his plan, but it was only after much urging that they reluctantly agreed to help him. Then the village elders had to be won over, but finally the cage that had housed so many pretty victims was brought from the crypt of the church, and the dog Devil was coaxed by a piece of raw mutton to enter through the door. Within minutes the cage had been strapped shut, and the four village men, with Harvey Trembath following, made their way up the mountain to the granite burial chamber. Just outside the entrance they set the cage down, all four of the young men refusing to stay a moment longer at that haunted spot and hurrying down the mountainside again as though pursued by a whole troop of hobgoblins. Harvey patted the dog, then covered the cage with a woven black cloth. To the wooden bar holding fast the door he tied one end of a string and, holding the other end of this string, he retreated into the darkness of the burial chamber.

Exactly at midnight there came the same terrible howling he had heard the night before, and there in the clearing were the green-eyed cats. Their evil-looking leader crept toward the cage as the others followed close behind, all eager to get at their prey. Just as the huge brute reached out to draw the cloth aside, Harvey tugged the string so that, as the cloth fell, so did the door imprisoning Devil. With a roar and a bound the dog was out, straight into the cats who were rigid with fear and astonishment.

Pandemonium reigned as with screams and curses the cats tried to escape. Harvey dashed out of the chamber with his heavy stick held high, kicking at the spitting cats as he tried to reach the spot where the dog and the monster who ruled the tribe wrestled and fought. Already the beast was changing back into a witch, and he knew that if she once managed to materialize into human form, the dog's teeth would bite only empty air and his trusty stick would pass straight through her. As he reached her, the other cats bit at his legs, but ignoring the pain he brought the heavy stick down with all his force on the cat-head of the witch. Already the rest of her body was human, but the head was always the last to change, and Harvey had struck in the nick of time.

As the blow fell, each and every cat uttered one long piercing scream. Then, as the leader rolled over dead, she and all the rest of the evil tribe shriveled and shriveled smaller and smaller until suddenly, when they were the size of mice, all of them started to twirl like tops, faster and faster. First one and then another smoked, then burst into flames with the friction, until there were thirteen little fires, each burning and crackling. As Harvey and the dog stood watching, the fires went out, and all that was left were thirteen small piles of ash. At that moment came a sudden unexpected gust of wind so that Harvey closed his eyes against the dust. When he opened them again, no trace of the witches could be seen. All around him birds were singing and the mountain felt at peace.

The young Cornishman took the brave dog back to his master amid the rejoicing of all the village. The bal-maiden whose life he had saved came shyly out of her parents' cottage and knelt and kissed his hand. Already the villagers were setting out trestle tables in the square for the feast of a lifetime. The witches had claimed their last victim and would trouble them no more. And Harvey and the prettiest girl in the village were already in love, which made the ending even happier!

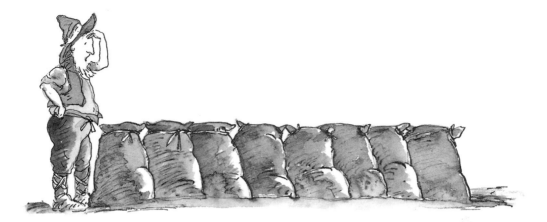

The Piskie Threshers

Long, long ago, before threshing machines were thought of, a certain poor farmer who lived near Chysauster in West Penwith went to his barn one spring morning and was astonished to find that an extraordinary amount of his grain had been threshed during the night. He had been threshing himself the previous day but had only managed the usual two bags of grain. Now a whole row of no less than eight well-filled sacks stood in a neat row along one wall of the barn.

For some time he stood there scratching his head in surprise and wondering how such an event could have occurred, the thought gradually coming that the little people might be responsible. But when he went back to the farmhouse and told his wife, she shook her head and refused to entertain any such thought. It was a joke he had made up to surprise her, she said. Even when he took her, grumbling and muttering, out to the barn and pointed to the bags of grain, she said he had worked harder than he thought and had threshed and filled the sacks himself.

"I tell 'ee it's the piskies' doing'!" the farmer said.

"There hasn't been a piskie in Chysauster since old Gran died, and that's nigh on twenty years!" his wife insisted.

Nothing he could say would convince her, but the more the farmer

45

thought of the matter, the more sure he was that the little people had come back. That night, when his wife was fast asleep, he quietly dressed himself and stole downstairs. It was a fine moonlit night, and as he put his head out of the door, he could hear, from the direction of the barn, the click-clack of the flail. Not just one flail but several. Clickity, clackity, clickity, clackity, click! A short pause, then again—clickity, clackity, clickity, clackity, click!

Hardly daring to breathe, he crept stealthily over to the barn door. Looking through a chink in the wood, he saw not one but three little fellows. Each was clad in a worn and tattered suit of green, and each was wielding his flail with astonishing vigor. They were beating the sheaves of grain with blows so rapid that his eyes could scarcely follow the strokes. At each short pause they wiped their foreheads, then set to work again. Clickity, clackity, clickity, clackity, click! Clickity, clackity, clickity, clackity, click! And the chaff rose in clouds, and the grain mounted in golden piles in a manner that made the farmer's heart glow with pleasure.

Minutes later he was creeping back up to his bedroom to awaken his wife and tell her all he had seen. Despite her protests he made her come over to the window, gently opened it, and with his arm around her shoulders told her to listen in the quiet of the night. There was no mistaking the sound. It was gentle and distant to be sure, but the wooden clatter of flails was borne on the wind.

"It be true then, John!"

"True enough, Nora."

The next morning, after they had both gone to the barn and smilingly counted yet another eight brimming sacks, they put their heads together to think of a way they could best show their gratitude to the hardworking little piskies. It was Nora who came up with an idea: Why not make each of them a new green suit? After all, the little men were practically in rags and tatters!

Within an hour the farmer was back home from Penzance with a bolt of fine green cloth tied to his saddle, and in less time than it takes to tell the tale Nora was busy with scissors and needle and thread. All day she worked, stopping only once for a bite of meat pie and a drink of tea, and

just as dusk was falling there was a little green suit laid out and ironed. But only one little green suit — there had been no time to make more — and before the moon was up John had placed it on the three-legged milking stool in the barn to await the arrival of the three little piskies. Pinned to it was a card with the words, "More tomorrow."

John and his wife went to bed early that night. Once again they listened at the window, but this time they heard what sounded like twittering and squeaking noises that went on for a long time. Then, just as they were about to clamber into bed, came the familiar clickity, clackity, clickity, clackity, clickity, clackity, click, but not so fast or so loud as before.

"I'm 'opin' they didn't quarrel over who 'ad what," said Nora, but her husband was already asleep.

Both of them were up soon after dawn and went immediately to the barn. Sure enough, the little green suit was gone, but this time there were only five filled sacks and a small heap of grain in the center of the threshing floor.

"It's still a lot of grain," said John, but Nora was already hurrying back to the farmhouse to her scissors and needle and thread.

That night another suit was finished and placed with its card saying, "More tomorrow," and once again the sounds of quarreling were heard coming from the barn. The next morning the new little green suit was gone, and there were only two and a half filled sacks standing by the wall.

"They're not trying so 'ard as before," said Nora, "but I'll make the last poor mite a suit all the same." And she hurried off to the farmhouse to her scissors and needle and thread.

That afternoon, when the suit was finished, John placed it in the barn as before, but this time there was no need for any notice to be pinned to it. He was determined to see what happened when it was found, so as soon as dusk fell he crept out to the barn and hid himself so that he could see through a chink in the wood. There was the suit just where he had placed it, and in less than five minutes a little piskie suddenly appeared as if from nowhere. The little man danced over to the suit and held it out at arm's length as he jibbered and jabbered with pleasure. Off came his ragged jacket and on went the smart new trousers. With one click of his fingers he conjured a magic mirror out of thin air before which he

twisted and turned to see himself to the best advantage, at the same time singing a song in Cornish English:

> "Piskie fine, and piskie smart,
> Piskie now is glad at heart,
> No more threshing farmer's grain,
> No more toil and no more pain,
> Piskie now will fly away!"

As the farmer blinked in surprise, the little fellow disappeared, leaving the sacks unfilled.

Nora only shook her head when John told her what he had seen, knowing what the bolt of cloth had cost and how hard she had worked to cut and sew each suit to shape. Her husband would have to thresh what remained of the grain himself, but tomorrow they could think about that. She would give him a hand herself, so she said, "Come 'ee up to bed to get our rest."

The sun was up before they walked together to the barn and pushed open the creaking door. The unfilled sacks were lying on the earthen floor, but on the three-legged milking stool was a leather purse with its lace tied tight. Nora looked at John, and John looked at Nora. His hand trembled so much he couldn't untie the knot, and she snatched the purse from him, unlaced the mouth, and tipped it up. A stream of golden sovereigns cascaded down at their feet, and they fell on their knees with tears of gratitude wetting their cheeks.

They were, after all, very poor people and had been poor all their lives, but now Nora could have the spinning wheel she had always longed for, while her hardworking husband could have the boots he needed so badly and maybe a brand-new plow!

"Bless the little people," said Nora. "Bless their little 'earts!"

The Mermaid of Zennor

It happened long, long ago, in the days when Neptune still held his court deep beneath the tranquil waters of the Sea of Japan. One night a fiery comet lit the sky as bright as the snow capping Mount Fuji. Then the sea trembled so fiercely that even the sea serpents dived to the deepest caves, while Neptune's castle of pinnacled coral swayed first to the right and then to the left before it toppled sideways in a swirling cloud of sand. Of the sixty-eight mermaids who swam attendance on the Lord of the Seas only three escaped, and two of these lost their magic combs and mirrors.

The youngest and by far the prettiest was Miranda, who could dimly remember later being trapped in the heart of a giant tsunami–a tidal wave–that swept her into the path of the Gulf Stream. Only after the tsunami had left her behind did Miranda open her sea-green eyes as the warmth of the stream revived her. She felt for her mirror and comb–a mermaid's most prized possessions–combed back the golden strands from her face, and peacefully floated. She was too exhausted to care where the Gulf Stream took her. Her mirror of mother-of-pearl and her comb of milk-white coral, found only in the deepest recesses of the South China Sea, she tucked firmly into the belt of woven seaweed that circled her slim waist.

Soon she realized that her tail was sore, and she could feel with her hand the places where scales had been rubbed away as she squeezed out of the ruins of Neptune's castle. So for several days she slept fitfully at her favorite depth of five fathoms, occasionally diving to the seabed for sponges. On these she squeezed iodine from the seaweed, rubbing the sore places on her tail until the pain had gone.

The day came when the Gulf Stream seemed to be flowing so slowly that Miranda became frightened that her food would all be gone before she once more reached a rocky shore. In her most respectful voice she asked the favor of a tow from a troop of sea horses who were just then overtaking her with a series of shrill little neighs. Their leader listened politely as she explained that the state of her tail made swimming difficult in the extreme, and he kept bobbing his head in sympathy. By the time she had told of the fate of her many sisters and cousins and how she herself had barely escaped disaster, many of the sea horses were in tears. Miranda herself repressed a sigh (mermaids cannot cry). Then she turned on her back as each of the little sea creatures took a strand of her long golden hair in the curl of his horny tail before commencing the tow in fanlike formation.

She had long since lost track of time, and how long the journey with
the sea horses took she could not tell, but her worries increased as she
gradually ate her way through her belt of seaweed. At last only two
strands were left–one forming a thin belt to hold her mirror and comb,
the other clutched in her hand. This was the strand she was determined
to plant and grow as soon as she found a new home.

By this time she was able to swish her tail gently to and fro to assist the
sea horses, the pain being completely gone where the newly grown scales
were gleaming. Then some eels who had joined the party called out that
they were approaching Land's End. Was she for turning left or right?
"Left!" shouted Miranda, delighted that land was at last in sight. All the
sea horses crowded around to say good bye, and she gave each a single
golden strand of hair as a remembrance.

She was on her own again, gliding beneath the waves, sensing the

rocky steadfastness of the wild Cornish coast and keeping it always on her right. As she rounded Cape Cornwall, she paused briefly to release the inmates of several lobster pots. Then she was off again rounding Gurnard's Head, as a dozen claws waved their thanks. The westering sun was sinking beneath the far horizon as Miranda swam thankfully inshore, entering the sandy-bottomed haven of Pendour Cove as gulls and ravens wheeled and circled their windswept roosts high on the cliffs above her.

She plucked at the beds of seaweed as she came close inshore; strange

and foreign kelp it seemed to her, totally unlike her Japanese *nori*. She amused herself by popping the seaweed bulbs between her fingers, following the bubbles as they escaped to the surface, and nibbling uncertainly at the fronds. The taste was strange, but she forced herself to eat, seeking out the tenderest and youngest shoots until she felt her hunger fade. Then she sought a resting place and found a cave just below the low tide mark, at the foot of a towering granite wall the villagers called the Horse's Back on account of the narrow ridge where the herring gulls nested. The cave was dark with seaweed and soft with drifted sand, and here she made a nest and curled her tail around her body before she fell asleep.

The next day was a Sunday, and it was late in the morning before Miranda, by a single slow flick of her tail, broke surface in Pendour Cove and windmilled her tresses so that the drops flew. A fat gray Atlantic seal, sunning itself quietly, looked on disapprovingly and edged its seal pup nearer as Miranda splashed water its way and cheekily put out her tongue. Then in the light offshore wind she heard the sound of bells.

Mermaids love music, and most of them can sing alluringly. Like all sea creatures, they have acute hearing, so she had no difficulty in following the words of the distant choir. Then came the voice of the soloist, his fine tenor tinged with a Cornish accent, and even for a Celt his singing was exceptional. It intrigued Miranda, and she automatically reached for her comb, using the still waters of a rock pool rather than her mirror as she burnished her golden tresses. Then she moved in a series of seallike flops across the sand to where the stream from the valley cascaded in its final swoop to the sea like a gray horse's tail. As she pulled herself upright, the spray covered her figure, and she emerged at the head of the waterfall looking like any pretty young girl, her tail seeming like a close-fitting full-length skirt of emerald green.

Zennor Churchtown lay higher up the valley through which the little river wound its way. The village was dominated by the square tower of the church, which was built of granite, like every cottage and outbuilding in the hamlet. Its churchyard overlooked the rough tangle of gorse and tamarisk that constituted the village green, cut through by the river as it left the town to flounce its way in a series of white-skirted falls down to the final plunge through the cliffs that edged the cove. It was forever a busy stream, peopled by trout and freshwater creatures the water birds sought out as they patrolled the bed. Herons stood sentry every hundred yards and one rose with a shriek and a flurry of outstretched wings as Miranda commenced her journey up toward the town. She paused as she came in sight of the clanking waterwheel at Eglosmeor Mill, but the miller and his wife, like all the rest of the village, were in their Sunday best and seated in the church, listening to the vicar drone his weekly sermon. Miranda watched a pair of courting otters scrambling up the steplike waterfalls, then squealing with delight as the water cascaded over them, washing them back down into the stream. "Come and try it!" they urged laughingly as they beckoned her with their flippers, but Miranda shook her head, telling them she was far too heavy and besides it wasn't ladylike.

She set off again, pausing to rest on a seat of flat slate and leaving it marked with the outline of her wet behind. She kept always to the river, snaking her way up the falls and through the deeper water of the level pools, the music from the church urging her on so that she reached the pool below the roofed gate of the churchyard a little out of breath. There the boughs of the tamarisk hung low, and she reached for a branch to pull herself upright, finally taking a precarious stance on her tail fins. She closed her eyes and concentrated on changing her form as the voices of the choir, famous throughout the whole of West Penwith, mingled with the sigh of the wind, the tenor of the soloist rising high above the rest.

When she finally opened her eyes, the wealth of golden hair, which had been her crowning glory, had all but disappeared, only a wisp peeping out from beneath the wide-brimmed hat that now magically adorned her head. The rest of her body was hidden by a dark green velvet dress exquisitely embroidered with thousands of seed pearls, while at her throat hung a necklace of sky-blue lapis lazuli.

Miranda made her way with little shuffling steps to the porch, entering the church noiselessly to hover behind a pillar at the back. As she gazed at the rustic congregation, the sunlight warmed the stained glass so that the church was flooded with multicolored light. At that moment Mathey Trewella finished reading the lesson and took his place at the head of the choir. He turned to face Miranda as she slid out from behind the pillar. She knew now whose voice it was that had enchanted her, and she smiled and willed the handsome young Cornishman to return her smile. Those near him turned to follow his gaze, and then the music struck up again. His voice was answered by hers, the two seeming to fill the church with a radiance of sound so that the rest of the congregation gradually fell silent as Mathey's and Miranda's voices intertwined. Only the deaf old priest, nodding and mumbling in the pulpit, seemed unmoved, waking with a start to give the final blessing.

The curious villagers remained silent as they filed out, but once outside they voiced their astonishment at the sight of the beautifully adorned lady who had appeared so mysteriously in their midst. Mathey made sure he was the last to leave. He stopped beside her as Miranda laid

a hand on his sleeve, then blushed as he stammered thanks for her praise. What did he do? she asked him.

"Carpenter and joiner, ma'am, like my father before me." He pointed to the half-finished screen, dominated by a large crucifix, at the entrance to the church, telling her he had worked on it alone. "It's kindly, ma'am, to interest yourself in the likes o' me." When she smiled and gently bowed her head, he clutched tightly at his cap and bowed himself. Then the door clanged and he was gone.

Miranda knew she had only minutes to change her form, for she could feel that her tail was drying and stiffening beneath her skirt. With villagers around, there was no time to reach the stream, so she moved awkwardly forward to the granite baptismal font and pulled herself up so that she sat on its edge. Then she closed her eyes tightly and willed herself to grow small.

Within seconds her costly velvet dress had dissolved and disappeared, as had her hat, releasing her golden tresses so that they swept down toward her glistening tail. As she became smaller and smaller, she willed herself to tadpole size, turning as she did so to slide down into the font. With a sigh, she felt the water closing over her.

From that time onward the strange and beautiful lady appeared each Sunday at Zennor church, always arriving well after the final prayer—though nobody could remember actually *seeing* her leave. Her voice and that of Mathey Trewella would inevitably mingle in duets of entrancing harmony so that the rest of the congregation fell silent, listening as they sang. Each Sunday saw the intricately carved screen come nearer and nearer to completion. And the miller and his wife knew by now that when they returned to the slate seat there was sure to be the imprint of a wet behind gradually drying in the sun. But they were careful never to mention the fact to anyone.

Then came the day in November when sea mist gentled its way up the valley. When Willi Craze turned from cutting furze bushes on Trewey Hill, all the village nestled under a blanket of white. The topmost turrets of the square-towered church stood clear above the cottony snow, black against the sheeted moon. An owl hooted in its glide from the old chimney where the miners worked the tin, so that Willi shuddered and urged his donkey home to Lady Downs.

The village was asleep, but the sound of chipping and chiseling came from the church, where Mathey was carving the final petal on the last of the roses that climbed the oaken screen. Finally he sighed and straightened, then stood back to assess the labor of many months. He sensed she was there before she spoke, turning his lantern so that the shadows danced.

"It's only me, Mathey."

She smiled as she moved toward him, and once again he detected the scent of the sea as his eyes sought the hem of her dark green dress. His hands shook slightly as she asked him to turn the lamp so she could see the village faces he had carved on the screen. Then she turned slowly back toward him, linking her fingers in his so that he felt the chill of her

skin. With her other hand she tilted his chin so that for the first time he looked directly into her sea-green eyes. As he moved to clasp her, she stepped lightly back.

"Carve my likeness on the end of this pew, my dear, before we leave."

He nodded obediently and groped for his chisels, stooping to lift the

flat-ended pew as she turned the lantern higher. The smell of the sea came stronger as she willed herself to become a mermaid again, and her hair draped down her back like a golden curtain. In one hand she held her mirror and in the other her comb as she posed, bare breasted, so that he fell to carving like one possessed, chipping away ceaselessly as the minutes slid by. Dawn was breaking as he reached the final scales on her fishlike tail.

It was the sexton who discovered the newly carved bench end when he opened the church door next morning, with the lamp beside it burned out and the floor covered with wood chips. He had left the font half full of water in preparation for a christening, but it was now almost dry. When he went to look for Mathey Trewella, his mother reported that his bed had not been slept in, but the search did not start in earnest until the early evening. That night, and for days afterward, the villagers searched every cliff and cove for miles around without finding the slightest trace of Mathey. Only later did people begin to link his disappearance with the fact that the mysterious lady never again appeared in church.

It was nearly two years later that the schooner *Endeavor* anchored in Pendour Cove, having been sent there by the Admiralty to investigate a perplexing growth of Japanese kelp, an exotic species of seaweed found nowhere else in Europe. It was feared that it might spread to choke harbors as far away as Penzance and Falmouth.

Within minutes of the anchor going down, a golden-haired mermaid rose close alongside and hailed the ship. Would the captain be so kind as to trip his anchor? The fluke was resting on the door of her dwelling, and she was anxious to return to her husband. The captain saluted and gave immediate orders for all sails to be set and the anchor weighed. Sailors never argue with a mermaid.

The crew crowded the rail as the sloop gathered way, and some of them shouted a greeting as the mermaid rose half out of the water holding her little merboy aloft. She waved the baby's hand, then turned on her back and kissed and cuddled the child, as she talked in a language strange to their ears and whose words were lost on the wind.

The Miser and the Little People

There once lived in the village of St. Just, not far from the Land's End, a mean and covetous old miser named Pierce Gaveston. Rich as he was, he craved more wealth, and to that end he had made up his mind to visit the playground of the little people, a grass-covered hill called the Gump about a mile from the village.

Many of the good old people in this remote part of Cornwall had been permitted to witness the revels of the little people, which took place on the Gump during the time of the harvest moon, in September. For years they had delighted their grandchildren with tales of the songs they had heard there and the marvelous sights they had seen. To some of them the fairies had actually given small but valuable presents made of pure gold, but woe to anyone who tried to steal anything from their hoards of precious metals and jewels. The thief's luck would be bad from that day on, so few were foolhardy enough to try.

However, tales of fairy gold tantalized old Pierce, and he resolved that by boldly taking certain chances he could steal some gold and get away with it. Some said afterward that thoughts of the gold had addled his brain. However, be that as it may, on a night of the full harvest moon Pierce set out for the Gump, walking silently on the grass and moving as quickly as he dared.

As he reached the hill, he suddenly heard music of the most ravishing kind. It appeared to surround him—music from instruments not of this earth, or so he thought, for he recognized not one of them, and all the tunes were new. It seemed the music was coming from the ground beneath his feet, when suddenly there was a crash louder than cymbals, and the hill before him opened.

All was now ablaze with many-colored lights, lights of every hue and description, hanging from bushes and trees and with very tiny ones on every blade of grass. The ground glowed as Pierce stood there petrified, for out of the opening in the hill marched a host of spriggans, hundreds of them, it seemed. They were followed by an immense number of little musicians playing on every type of instrument, while behind them came troop after troop of soldiers, each troop holding aloft its banner, which appeared to spread itself so as to display its colors and symbols without the assistance of even a breath of wind.

The various groups arranged themselves in order, some here and some there, while several hundred of the most grotesque and ugly spriggans formed a circle around the spot on which Pierce Gaveston was standing. At first the old man thought they were about to attack him, but nothing happened, and he consoled himself with the thought that he could jump over their heads and easily escape, for none of them was more than six inches high.

The vast array of little people having disposed themselves into orderly groups, there next came a crowd of servants bearing vessels of silver and gold, goblets cut out of diamonds, rubies, and other precious stones. There were others laden almost to overflowing with the richest meats, pastries, preserves, and fruits. Presently the ground was covered with little tables, which the servants set and arranged before falling back to stand in respectful rows.

The brilliance of the scene nearly overpowered the old miser, and no sooner had he become used to the sight than the lights suddenly brightened several fold. Out of the hill came crowding hundreds of little people, each arrayed in the most costly attire, while the odor of flowers, sweeter and more delicious than any Pierce had ever smelled, filled the

air. The little people were talking in a language unknown to him, with crowds of their own tiny children laughing and playing. Some were strewing flowers on the hillside, and as soon as these touched the ground, each and every one of them took root and grew.

Then there came line upon line of little men clothed in green and gold, carrying a forest of banners. Behind them, seated on thrones carried above the heads of the men, came a young prince and princess who positively blazed with jewels. There was much ceremonial marching to and fro, but eventually the platform on which the thrones rested was gently lowered onto a mound upon the Gump, which had by this time been transformed into a hillock of roses and lilies and masses of exotic blooms. One by one the richly attired little people filed past their prince and princess, bowing or curtsying before moving on to stand waiting behind their seats. When all had saluted their rulers, the prince made a signal, and with one accord all took their seats at the heavily laden tables. The prince's personal servants, in splendid liveries, placed before the two of them tables laden with solid gold plates and all kinds of delicious food and drink, and at another signal the feast began.

Well, thought the old miser to himself, now is my time! He crouched down and began slowly to crawl to where the prince and princess sat in all their glory, making his way between the revelers and never noticing that hundreds of spriggans had secretly thrown little strings around him and that they still held the ends of the threads. The presence of the old man did not seem in the least to discompose the hundreds of little feasters, who carried on with their meal as though he were not there at all. All the time he was getting closer to the head table with its gold and jewels, going around to the back of the hill so that he could take them from behind.

At length he reached the desired spot, a place where all was dark and gloomy, contrasting with the blaze of light where the diners sat. He crawled like a serpent on his stomach until he was directly behind the prince and princess. Slowly he raised himself to his knees; then, taking off his hat, he bent forward to place it over the royal pair and the gold-laden table. He was just about to bring down his hand to scoop everything up in his hat when a sudden shrill whistle rang in his ears and his arm instantly stiffened so that he could move not a muscle. His hand was fixed powerless in the air, and everything went dark around him.

Whir! Whir! Whir! as if a swarm of bees were attacking him. Then every limb felt as if hundreds of pins and needles had been stuck into it. He tried to move, but he seemed chained to the ground; then a sudden shove, and he was rolling down the mound. He lay on his back at the bottom. His outstretched arms and legs seemed to be roped tightly to the

ground. As the pinpricks continued, he tried to cry out, but no sound came. He was not only paralyzed but struck dumb as well. While lying there in this sad plight, he felt what seemed to be a horde of insects running over his body, and then, by the light of the moon he saw standing on his nose one of the smallest spriggans, not much bigger than a dragonfly. Urged on by the others, the spriggan started jumping up and down on the end of Pierce's nose, screeching with laughter as it did so.

How long this would have gone on one can only guess, for suddenly the prince shouted, "Away, away, I smell the day!" Upon hearing this, the entire army of little people gathered all the gold and jewels and tables and chairs and everything they had brought with them and marched back inside the hill. No sooner had the final little figure vanished from view than there came a single clap of thunder and the hillside was sealed. All that remained to be seen was the grassy knoll the locals called the Gump.

The old miser lay as they had left him, still unable to move hand or foot. Then a cock crowed and it was dawn. As the sun rose, Pierce could see that he was tied to the ground by hundreds and hundreds of gossamer threads, as thin as spiders' webs. They were glistening like diamonds with the early morning dew, but no way could he break them. He heard the distant church clock striking all the hours until noon, and then, at the first stroke of twelve, the threads fell away and he was free.

Never again did he attempt to spy on the little people, and for fear of their vengeance he sold his house in St. Just at a giveaway price and left the very next day for Truro. What happened to him after that only the spriggans know!

The Old Woman and the Spriggans

Many years ago there lived an old woman whom many called a witch. Her lonely cottage stood in a wild and isolated Cornish valley beside a rocky stream. She was said to be the widow of a tin miner killed years ago in a fall down a shaft.

Whether they presumed upon her solitude or whether the old lady had given them some inducement is not now known, but many of the spriggans of Trencrom Hill were in the habit of meeting almost every night in her cottage to divide their plunder. Old Flora usually slept, or at least pretended to sleep, during the visits of the spriggans, as these little elves are called in Cornwall. When they left, they always placed a small coin on the table by her bedside, and with these, saved over many weeks, she was able to buy not merely food and clothing but many little things that were luxuries to one in her position.

There was one thing she longed for above all else, but she knew that even if she saved every penny piece for all of two years there would still not be enough to buy it. Once, in St. Ives, she had seen a neat little cottage standing empty and forlorn. She knew her few sticks of furniture would look fine in it, and maybe she could buy a stick or two more. From her own cottage she had too far to walk, or rather, hobble, for now that she was old she was unsteady on her legs. To live in a fine town like St. Ives, close to the marketplace, was all she now really desired. But the cottage had been priced at thirty pounds, a sum old Flora could hardly imagine, much less count up to, so there her dream must rest.

However, thinking of her future prospects, living miles from the nearest habitation, she finally resolved on a plan that might make her dream come true. But she resolved to bide her time until the spriggans had an unusually large amount of plunder to divide up, and the weeks went by as she lay every night listening to their chattering and squeaking.

One evening in early June each and every one of the spriggans arrived loaded with gold and jewelry. As usual, they tipped it into a heap on the old woman's floor, where it gleamed and glistened as Flora looked on with covetous eyes. But this particular evening the spriggans seemed unable to divide the treasure amicably, and before long a violent quarrel broke out. Some of the little thieves were so angry with the other elves' choice of jewelry that they actually began to hit each other and wrestle on the floor.

"Now's my chance!" said Flora to herself, and huddling under the bedclothes she very adroitly managed to turn her shift—that is, she turned her nightgown inside out—a task she had secretly practiced many times. Having completed this unfailing charm, which was proof against any magic the spriggans might try to use against her, Flora rolled from under the bedclothes off the bed and stretched her poor old body over the treasure.

"It's mine now!" she shrieked. "It's mine!"

The startled spriggans were already scampering for their lives up the chimney and away as their chief vainly tried spell after spell. Then he, too, bolted like the rest.

Flora was too wise to stay another day in her lonely cottage, for the turned shift was proof only until the next Sunday. At first light she was up and away, the gold and jewels tied tightly in her shawl, limping her way slowly along the rab-covered coastal path to St. Ives. When she reached the Stennack Hill, she paused and looked back at the desolate moors behind her, vowing never, never to return.

That very day, to everyone's surprise, she bought her snug little cottage, sent men to fetch her few sticks of furniture, and busied herself making her new home spic-and-span. Now that she had so much money no one even thought of calling her a witch anymore, and she lived like a gentlewoman to the end of her days.

Duffy and the Devil

It was cider-making time in West Penwith, and Squire Lovel of Trewoof decided to ride into St. Buryan Churchtown to recruit a few sturdy lads and maidens to gather the apples and carry them to the cider mill. He would pay them sixpence a day, and at the end of their stint he would let each one take home a tankard of his best cider. He was a generous man, and he believed in rewarding hardworking servants in a way they appreciated.

As he rode at a dignified gait through the streets of the village his attention was drawn to the noise of quarrelsome voices, one in a shrill treble and the other crying, proceeding from Janey Chygwin's door. The squire rode up to the cottage and saw the old woman beating her stepdaughter Duffy about the head with the charred skirt of her gown, in which she had been carrying out the ashes. She made such a dust that the squire and the girl were nearly choked and blinded by wood ashes.

"Hold on there, Janey!" cried the squire. "What's the to-do with you and Duffy?"

"This lazy hussy of a daughter o' mine," shouted Janey, "spends all of 'er time chasin' the boys! She never boils the porridge, cleans the 'ouse, knits the stockings, or spins the yarn! She's good for nothin', so she is!"

"Don't believe 'er, your honor," shouted Duffy. "My knitting and spinning is the best in the parish."

Now, Duffy was a very pretty young miss, and while the squire went around the village to do his hiring, he soon came to the conclusion that she would make a most desirable addition to the staff at Trewoof Hall. With all his apple gatherers selected, he rode back to the cottage and found peace had been restored. Upon asking the old woman if she would let her stepdaughter go, she was nodding her head even before taking the half a guinea he passed her.

"I want her to help in the house and do the spinning," Lovel told her.

"A pretty spinner she is!" said old Janey with a smile.

"We'll soon see about that," said the squire when he and Duffy had left the cottage. "Janey's glad to be quits of thee, I see, and thou'lt not be sorry to leave her, so jump up behind me, Duffy."

Squire Lovel's old housekeeper was almost blind, one of her eyes having been put out by a witch many years ago, so she was glad to have help with her spinning and knitting. No sooner was supper over than she took Duffy up to the room where the wool was kept and told her to commence her work and bring down a finished specimen in the morning.

To tell the truth, Duffy was hopeless at both spinning and knitting, and there was no way she was going to learn now. The garret was piled from the floor to the ceilingbeams with fleeces of wool. Duffy looked despairingly at them and then sat down at the spinningwheel and began to cry.

"Curse the spinning and knitting! The devil may spin and knit for the squire for all I care!"

Scarcely had Duffy uttered these words than she heard a rustling noise behind some of the stacks of wool and out walked a strange-looking little man with a remarkable pair of eyes that seemed to send out flashes of light. He was dressed all in black, and as he walked toward the girl, she heard a knock at each step as though some object trailed behind him and was striking the floor.

"Duffy, dear," said the little gentleman, "I'll do all the spinning and knitting for thee."

"Thank'ee, kindly," said Duffy when she had recovered from her

astonishment, "thank'ee kindly."

"Duffy, dear, a lady shall you be."

"Thank'ee, your honor," said Duffy dropping him a curtsy.

"But, Duffy, dear, remember that I make one condition," said the strange little man—even stranger now, thought Duffy, for she had just noticed among the thick curls of his black hair a pair of small curved horns—"one condition only, but it is not to be broken. At the end of three years I will come to claim you—unless you can find out my name."

"Your name?"

The little man nodded. "Yes, my dear, you must tell me my true name and no other, and you will only have three guesses."

Duffy dropped him another curtsy.

"As for tonight's spinning, you will find all you require under the black ram's fleece."

"Thank'ee kindly, sir."

As he turned to go, she could see the end of the spiked tail protruding from beneath the back of his cloak, but when she looked again he had vanished. It was then that she noticed a faint smell of sulfur in the air. By the time it had cleared, Duffy was already asleep in a bed of fleeces.

The next morning, there, sure enough, was the large hank of wool neatly spun into yarn, and when the girl showed the work to the old housekeeper and the squire, they both declared it was the finest yarn they had ever seen. They thought she must have been up half the night spinning it, and Duffy certainly said nothing to make them think otherwise.

That day she helped with the housework and was given a proper bedroom to herself, but the following morning the squire asked her to go up to the wool storeroom and knit the yarn into stockings. Duffy idled the morning away and at noontime lifted the black ram's fleece where she had placed the hank, and there, ready for use, was a fine pair of stockings. When the squire and the housekeeper saw and handled them, they were amazed. The stockings were as fine as silk yet seemingly as strong as leather!

Squire Lovel soon gave them a trial, and they wore so well that when he came in at night after a day's hunting, he declared that in the future he would wear only Duffy's stockings. He had hunted all day through brake and briar, furze and brambles, yet there was not so much as a scratch on his legs, and his feet were as dry as a bone.

Duffy had a rare time of it now: she could do exactly as she pleased and had only to wish for a thing for her wish to be granted. Most days she spent gossiping with the women at the mill, for a handful of village women always waited there for their grist to be ground, and they didn't sit silent. They would tell stories and pass on the latest scandal, and an itinerant old fiddler would often set to and play for a penny a time. It was then the girls and women danced together, and Duffy always among the leaders. On these occasions the women beat time on a "crowd," as it was called, "crowd" being Cornish for the miller's sieve covered with a tightly stretched sheepskin and used as a large tambourine.

Now, old Bet, the miller's wife, was a witch, and the fact that Duffy apparently worked so well at her spinning and knitting yet always found time to visit the gossips at the mill made her suspicious. One day Duffy proudly brought a pair of stockings to be examined and praised, the other women crowding around and exclaiming at their fine texture. Minutes later old Bet drew the girl aside.

"I know 'ow you does it, dearie!"

Duffy colored and said that she had been well trained to the task.

Bet sidled closer. "Your secret's safe enough with me, dearie, but I knows 'oo do 'elp you. You see, there's always a stitch down, always one unlocked. Anything 'e knits will carry that mark. One stitch dropped!" And old Bet laughed and cackled to herself.

"Don't thee tell, now, Bet!"

The old witch nodded and promised, and after that the two became the best of friends, Bet telling the girl she would do her best to help when the three years were up.

On Sundays the country people for miles around went to St. Buryan Church, many of them coming specially to look at the squire's new stockings about which many tales had been told. He stood there after the service at the churchyard gate, proudly displaying his legs. He told them he could hunt "through brambles and furze in all sorts of weather; my old shanks as sound as if bound up in leather!"

Duffy was now sought after by all the eligible young men of the county, but the squire, fearing to lose so pretty and useful a girl, proposed marriage himself and was accepted. According to the fashion at that time, young Duffy became Lady Lovel upon her marriage, but she was commonly known by her friends and neighbors as Duffy Lady.

Lady Lovel kept the devil hard at work. Stockings, bedding, fine underclothes, and much ornamental work, the like of which had never before been seen, was produced at her command, and she passed it all off as her own. Her own beautifully knitted skirts and dresses were the envy of all who beheld them, except old Bet, who just laughed and clapped her hands. It was with her that Duffy spent much of her spare time, and she passed hours at the mill learning the tricks and arts the old witch taught her. As for the squire, he hunted and gambled and drank and seemed to care not a jot about Duffy as long as she kept him well supplied with the clothes and household materials he ordered.

The three years were nearly at an end, and Duffy had tried every plan to find out the devil's name, but even with old Bet's help she had completely failed. She began to despair and dreaded the day the evil one would come to fetch her. Bet tried to cheer her up, telling her there was still time left and that her many dealings with the imps and fairies and the powers of darkness might yet yield some result. She would think of a plan before long.

Finally there was only one day left, and a white-faced Duffy pleaded with Bet to find a way out. They *must* discover the devil's name! Somehow, somehow, they *must*! Suddenly the witch clapped her hands, and broke into a smile. This is what Duffy Lady must do. Listen carefully.

Duffy Lady was to bring down to the mill that evening a large tankard of the strongest drink in the whole of the squire's winecellar. On no account was she to retire to bed before her husband returned from hunting, no matter how late he might be. And she was not to speak a word to him no matter what he said. Did she understand? She was simply to obey!

That evening the tankard of brandy was duly carried to the mill, and Duffy returned home full of trepidation to wait up for the squire. No sooner had she left the mill than old Bet came out with the "crowd" over her shoulders and the tankard in her hand. She shut the door, turned the watershoot aside to miss the millwheel, threw her red cloak around her, and away!

Duffy waited long and anxiously, and then, about midnight, the dogs arrived back home. Their mouths were covered with foam, and their tongues were hanging out. The servants declared they must have met the devil's hounds and fled home from the spot. Their mistress was now seriously alarmed. One o'clock struck, and still no squire, but before the clock struck the hour again, he was home and singing his head off like a crazy man:

"Here's to the devil,
With his wooden pick and shovel."

At first she thought he was drunk, but it appeared he was wild with some strange excitement.

"My dear Duffy," he said at last as he sat down, "you haven't smiled for some weeks past, but I'll tell 'ee something that will make you laugh, believe me! If you had seen what I have seen tonight, ha, ha, ha!"

80

"Here's to the devil,
With his wooden pick and shovel."

True to her orders Duffy said not a word, but allowed the squire to ramble on as he pleased. And at last he settled down to tell her the whole story of his adventure that night.

Apparently he had hunted the moors from Trove to Trevider, but had not flushed as much as a single hare. He was determined that, come what may, he would bring a brace back home. As night fell he went down to Lamorna Bottoms, then up Brene Downs, and just as he got to the Merry Pipers, as the ring of standing stones was called, out jumped as fine a hare as he had ever seen. Off went the dogs with the squire running after, and although time and again the squire almost had her in his sights, each time she sped away again. Finally she bolted into Fugoe Hole, a cave extending from the cliffs far underground, with the dogs

81

and the squire going after her, disturbing owls and bats so that the air rustled with their wings.

They came at last to a broad stretch of water, a deep pool, at which the dogs halted, then came bolting back, howling in fear. The squire tried to stop them, but they were off into the night, their howls getting fainter. Lovel paused and seemed to hear voices. He went to the edge of the pool and looked around the corner where the cave turned. There, before a glimmering fire, were the St. Levan witches in scores! Some were riding on ragwort, some on broomsticks, some on their three-legged stools. Among them was old Bet of the mill, with her home-made tambourine in one hand and the squire's own large leather bottle in the other.

Hardly daring to move, Lovel watched as the witches gathered to make their fire blaze, which it did with a strange blue flame. Then there was a sudden flash of light, and a strange little man appeared, dressed in black and holding his long forked tail high in the air. Old Bet immediately struck her "crowd" and beat out a tune:

> "Here's to the devil,
> With his wooden pick and shovel,
> Diggin' tin by the bushel,
> With 'is tail cocked up!"

Then the devil and all the witches danced in a circle, faster and faster, and each time the little man passed her, Bet held out the tankard and he took a long swig. The brandy seemed suddenly to have gone to his head, the squire told Duffy, beating his knee with excitement, for he was now staggering around instead of dancing. He roared with laughter and shouted out:

> "Duffy, my lady, you'll never know—what?
> That my name it is Terrytop, Terrytop—top!"

As the squire sang out these lines Duffy turned as pale as death, then red, then pale again, but she held her tongue and said nothing.

After the dance, all the witches made a ring around the fire, which

again flared up in blue flames. The devil danced through them without the least harm, though twice he fell flat on his back as the brandy took effect. The second time, the squire couldn't stop laughing, he told his wife, and even called out, "Well done, Old Nick!" Instantly there was pandemonium, the devil, with all the witches behind him, shooting up to the roof of the cavern, then through a hole under the sky. The fire disappeared, and only with difficulty did Lovel find his way back out. It was nearly an hour before he got back home.

"Why don't you laugh, Duffy?"

The girl permitted herself a smile, then with a nod of her head poured her husband a large mug of brandy and went up to bed.

There were still a few hours to go before the three years were up, for the time had been set at dawn the next day, so Duffy lay on the bed wishing her wishes and making the most of her time. Knitted things of every description appeared as if by magic, which of course it was, and she finally got up with her arms absolutely full and filled every chest and drawer in the house while the squire, having finished the brandy bottle, snored in his chair.

She had just gone up to the wool storeroom for the last of the knitted things when she noticed the blinds were letting in the day. There came a clunk, clunk, clunk behind her and a hand tapped her shoulder. Despite herself, Duffy gave a sudden start, knowing before she turned around who it was that stood there.

"Time's up, Duffy, my dear. Time's up."

The devil gave a mocking bow and crooked his finger for her to come away.

"I fear," said Duffy, rapidly regaining her composure, "that your country is a trifle too warm for me and might spoil my complexion."

"Enough of this," said the little man in black. "I've kept my part of the bargain, and I'm trusting a lady of your standing will keep her part of the bargain, too."

He made a step toward her, but Duffy held up her hand.

"But stay, sir! You've forgotten I'm allowed three guesses."

The devil smiled. "A waste of time, but go on. Tell me my name."

Duffy hesitated. "I say your name is . . . Lucifer."

84

The devil's lips curled in a grin as his tail turned up under his cloak. "That's one guess gone. Lucifer's no more than a servant to me in my country. A mere stoker, sweating it out with a shovel. Good at his job, mind!" He paused. "I'm waiting."

Duffy frowned and knit her brows. "Perhaps my lord's name is Beelzebub?"

The little man in black positively grinned. "Beelzebub? Me? Why he's no better than the other you mentioned. Just a common devil like all the rest but three. Come on, now, Duffy, give in and come with me."

"I've one guess left, your honor."

The devil was smiling broadly now, every now and then triumphantly licking his lips, his tail cocked high in the air behind him. "I haven't all day, my dear, so get it over with!"

Again Duffy hesitated, knitting her brows as though deep in thought.

"Well, sir, there's but one more name I can think of." She bit her lips and stared hard at the floor.

"Get on with it!"

"Might your lordship's name be . . . Terrytop?"

Instantly the devil's face contorted with anger and a strong smell of sulfur pervaded the room.

"Terrytop! Deny it if you dare!"

So great was the demon's rage that sparks of static crackled across his horns, and, making no attempt at concealment, he stamped his cloven hooves in anger. "Some cursed witch has told you this!"

"I'm right! I'm right!" And Duffy danced for joy, holding the hem of her beautifully knitted skirt as she circled the little man, her feet tapping and her eyes shining. "Goodbye, my lord. I'm sure you 'ave other business to attend to."

The devil was trying to control himself, muttering about three years of work for nothing and vowing vengeance on all and sundry.

"Never did I think to be beaten by a young minx like you." He fixed her with his piercing eyes. "I'm consoled by the thought that the pleasure of your company is merely postponed." He bowed low in mock courtesy, and as she blinked her eyes he disappeared.

Duffy wafted her hand before her face. "Pooh! What a stink!"

I wish at this point I could write the words "and they all lived happily

ever after," but within a month young Lady Lovel was left a widow, her squire having accidentally shot himself under somewhat mysterious circumstances. Apparently his trigger got caught in a bramble and fired the gun, though exactly how he came to be hit in the back of the head was never satisfactorily explained. The old housekeeper with her one and only eye died of shock soon after hearing the news, whereupon Duffy installed old Bet in her place, while Bet's daughter ran the mill.

From that day onward there was laughter and merrymaking at Trewoof Hall, and many a wild party was held there with music and dancing far into the night. Old Bet brought many of her friends from the witches' coven to what she called her "special occasions," much to the scandal of the surrounding parishes. The squire had left Duffy a wealthy woman, for the chest of gold in the best bedroom was now all hers, as well as the land and farms he owned. But she never married again.

What apprenticeship Duffy served in her witch's training was never revealed, but there were those in the village who swore they had seen her, bold as brass, swishing away from Trewoof Hall on her broomstick on her way to a meet. And the hares in the district increased alarmingly, though try as they might no one could catch one.

Yet she was kind to the humble folk, and many a golden guinea did she give at Buryan Feast and at Yuletide. Then one day, in her eighty-fifth year, she just vanished. The hall was searched from top to bottom, but to no avail. There was a strong smell of sulfur everywhere, which took days to clear. Some say they can smell it still each anniversary of the day Duffy vanished, but that's probably an old wives' tale.

The Shawl Ghost

Many years ago there lived in the little village of Trewey, in the far west of Cornwall, a poor and very old woman. She had no children or grandchildren of her own, but she cherished and loved a little girl called Alanna, the daughter of a neighbor. To the child she was always known as Aunt Kitty, and the little girl cried for many hours when her mother told her the old lady was dying.

Knowing her end was near, Aunt Kitty summoned her neighbor to her bedside and told her she had nothing of value to leave to the little girl she loved so much except a fine silk shawl. As a young woman it had been given to her by a sailor who had traveled to foreign parts. She had pledged him her heart, but when he next sailed away he was lost in a storm off Biscay and never returned. Alanna's mother promised to do as she was bid, but learning after the funeral that such a fine shawl could be worth as much as a guinea, she said nothing to her daughter and hid the shawl in a little pewter pot, which she sealed and buried under the stone-paved floor of their cottage.

A few evenings after the old woman's funeral, the child became restless in bed, then suddenly startled the household by bursting into shrieks as she pointed her finger to the far corner of the room. The others crowded around her and asked what had made her screech.

"Can't you see 'er? Can't you see 'er? There! Over there—it's Aunt Kitty with 'er face tied up in a white napkin and nothin' on 'er but a sheet!"

Night after night the old woman's ghost continued to haunt little Alanna, until her father, a strong man of great faith, picked up the child and took her outdoors. Almost immediately the little girl pointed across the garden, exclaiming, "There she is again!"

Her father for the first time saw the spirit, and although his face went white and there was a tremble to his hands, he walked toward it shouting: "In the name of goodness I command thee to answer why you 'ave come back to 'aunt this little child!"

The ghost of the old woman remained silent for several seconds. Then its lips began to move: "Because the shawl was not given to the child, I cannot rest."

"The shawl? What shawl?" asked the girl's father, for his wife had said nothing to him about the valuable gift.

Again the spirit spoke: "Because the shawl was not given to the child, I cannot rest."

The man stared at the ghost in silence, then nodded his head. "It shall be done, I promise you. Now depart in peace. As he spoke the words, the spirit of the old lady vanished as an owl swooped low over Trewey fields.

That same night the weeping mother dug up the pewter pot and handed it over to the child's father. He broke the sealing wax, took the tip of the silken shawl, and gradually pulled it forth into the lamplight. "This is for you, Alanna. Aunt Kitty told us to keep it safe." The girl nodded and gazed proudly at the shawl on her shoulders in the cracked old mirror on the wall.

All the Trewey folk were sure that no more would be seen or heard of the old woman's ghost. However, three days later, when the little girl was out on the moors playing Cornish hide-and-seek with several of her friends she vanished utterly and completely! Several of the children said that they saw her spirited away up and over the furze bushes, high over the haystacks, and all of them ran home to tell the tale breathlessly to their parents.

When darkness fell, many of the Trewey villagers gave up hope of ever again seeing the child alive, and when her father came back from searching the moors, shaking his head and close to tears, they crowded around Alanna's cottage to console the weeping mother. Then, suddenly, the girl was standing there among them with only one shoe on.

Questioned as to where she had been and how she had lost her shoe, the child answered that she didn't know. All she could remember was being whisked high in the air over the houses and haystacks until she gently descended to a strange churchtown with lots of trees. She found herself lying on a newly filled grave with the sound of singing in her ears. She saw nobody, but suddenly felt someone kiss her—a cold kiss that had her shivering as she was carried once again high in the air back to her own churchtown. And here she was!

From what the child had said, all the Trewey people thought she must have been spirited away to Ludgvan, for that was where the trees grew best. There were no trees on the Zennor-Morvah coast, for the storms and gales were fierce in their possession of the land, while on the soft south flank around Ludgvan and Penzance the hills broke the fury of the wind so that it could only sigh, or so it was said in Towednack. It was in Ludgvan that the old woman had been buried, for that was where her folk had their plot.

The next day several villagers, Alanna's mother and father among them, hurried over the moors to Ludgvan Churchtown to push open the old iron gate of the churchyard. There, in the far corner was Aunt Kitty's freshly dug grave, and as they reached it, the matter was put beyond any doubt. Alanna's missing shoe lay there on the soil. They turned away and left it where it lay so that the old woman might have something belonging to the little girl she loved, to put her to rest, as they said.

And so it proved. She has kept quiet from that day to this.

The Adventure of Cherry of Zennor

Old Winbroome lived with his wife and family in a little granite cottage of only two rooms and a loft on the cliffside of the valley leading down to Zennor Head. The old couple had half a score of children who were all born and reared in their isolated little home. They lived as best they could on the produce of a few acres of land, where they kept a goat or two and a pig and six geese. The heaps of limpet shells and periwinkles they used to strew their paths told how they scoured the rocks in Pendour Cove, but they had fish and potatoes most days, and pork and broth most Sundays. At Christmas and at Zennor Feast they always had roast goose, and even white bread and butter.

There was not a healthier and happier family in all the parish than old Winbroome's, and of them the healthiest and happiest and prettiest was surely their daughter Cherry. She could run, so they said, as fast as a hare and was ever full of frolic and mischief, but now that she was growing up, she had become discontented with life because for year after year her mother had promised her a new dress so that she might attend Morvah Fair as smart as the rest. But as each annual feast day dawned, her mother could only shake her head and say they were too poor to afford such a luxury. Perhaps next year.

When Cherry was sixteen, one of her friends in the village had a new dress smartly trimmed with silk ribbons. She told Cherry she had been over to Nancledra to hear the preaching and had ever so many sweethearts to bring her home. This was more than Cherry could bear, and she immediately declared to her mother that she was going up Trewey Hill to New Mill or perhaps even to Gulval to seek work as a servant so that she might have money to buy pretty dresses like other girls. Her mother pleaded with her to go only so far as Towednack so that she might have a chance to see her now and then on a Sunday.

"No, no!" said Cherry. "I'll never go and live in a parish where the one and only cow was so starved it ate the church bell rope, and where they can only eat fish and taties and conger-eel pie even on feast day and Christmas!"

The next morning Cherry tied up her few possessions in a bundle and bade farewell to her parents. Her old father said she must be bewitched and charged her to take care she wasn't carried off by sailors or pirates. Then he kissed her forehead and let her depart.

With her clothes tied up in a red kerchief fastened to a stick that she rested on her shoulder, Cherry turned but once to wave a last farewell as she stepped out up the valley to the rab-covered road that was to lead her to Gulval and fortune. Rab, as everybody knows, is the hard, yellow clay the villagers use to pave the lanes that lead to the wide, wide world and to St. Ives and Penzance and even to Truro, though few Cornish folk have been that far.

By the time she reached Lady Downs, as the high moors were called, Cherry was already feeling a little homesick, so she sat down by the milestone, with one of its hands pointing to Gurnard's Head and the other to New Mill, and shed a little tear. When she had dried her eyes, she was surprised to see a gentleman coming toward her, though she had looked this way and that across moors only minutes before and had spied only a mother donkey with its foal.

The gentleman wished her good morning and enquired where she was going on such a fine day with her bundle on a stick.

"I'm seeking to go into service, to save a penny or two to buy a fine

new frock such as they wear over in Penzance," said Cherry, dropping a curtsy and lowering her eyes.

"I never expected to meet with such luck as this," said the gentleman. "I left home this morning to seek a nice clean girl to keep house for me, and here you are!" He then told Cherry he had been recently left a widower and that he had one dear little son, of whom Cherry would have charge. She was the very girl he needed. She was pretty and clean, and he could see that her clothes were mended in such a neat and clever way that one could hardly tell where the patches began or ended.

He kept talking in this fashion, and all poor Cherry could say was, "Yes, sir! Yes, sir!" to everything, for she just could not understand all the long and hard words he used.

Away they went, he talking so kindly that Cherry had no notion how fast time was moving or how great a distance they had walked. They were now in lanes so shaded by trees that hardly a patch of sunshine came through. As far as she could see all was trees and flowers. Sweetbrier and honeysuckle perfumed the air, and the reddest of ripe apples hung down for the taking. A stream, with water as clear as crystal, crossed their path, but in an instant the gentleman had his arm around Cherry's waist and whisked her over so that no drop of water touched her shoes.

Then suddenly they were at a small wicket-gate leading into a garden so beautiful that Cherry could scarcely believe her eyes.

"Cherry, my dear, this is where you are to live."

She had never seen anything approaching this wondrous place for beauty. Flowers of every size and color were massed around her while fruit of all kinds was waiting to be picked. Even the birds seemed sweeter in song than any she had heard before, and as they opened the gate to enter they burst into a chorus of rejoicing. Cherry had heard her mother tell of enchanted places, and she thought surely this must be one of them.

It was then that a child appeared, a little boy about three years old, running toward them down the garden path, shouting, "Papa! Papa!" His eyes were so brilliant and piercing that Cherry could not stand their gaze and instinctively looked down. She thought she ought to greet her little charge, but before she could speak there came stumbling and

grumbling out of the house a most hideous old woman, who seized the child by the arm and dragged him back inside, at the same time casting a look at Cherry that seemed to pierce her like a gimlet. Seeing the girl look afraid, the master explained that this was his late wife's grandmother and that she would remain with them only as long as it took Cherry to learn her work and no longer, for she was old and ill-tempered and would have to go. The boy called her Aunt Aggie.

Muttering and grumbling Aggie did as she was told and prepared an appetizing supper to which Cherry did full justice, even though many of the foods were strange to her. Aggie then led her to the nursery where she was to sleep near the little boy. The old woman gave strict instructions that on no account was Cherry to open her eyes during the night, whether she slept or no, for she might see things she would not like. She was not to speak to the child all night. She was to rise at break of day, take the boy to a spring in the garden, wash him, and then anoint his eyes with an ointment that she would find in a crystal box in a cleft in the rocks. She was not on any account to touch her own eyes with it. At this the old crone shook a bony finger in Cherry's face and hissed the words again, "Don't touch your eyes with it, or it'll be the worse for you!"

"What'll I do next, then?" asked Cherry, and was told she must put back the crystal box exactly where she found it and then call for the cow.

"Call for the cow?"

"Like this, you little fool!" The old hag made a clucking noise with her tongue for Cherry to imitate, then told the girl to milk a full bucket and draw a bowl of milk for the boy's breakfast.

As soon as the old woman left them alone, Cherry, who was itching with curiosity, began to question the boy, but after every question he immediately stopped her with "I'll tell Aunt Aggie!" so that in the end she gave up.

Soon after dawn the next day, Cherry roused the boy and took him, as she had been told to do, into the garden. There she found the spring, which flowed out of a granite rock covered with ivy and beautiful mosses. She washed the child and then found the crystal box just where

Aggie had said it would be. Unscrewing the top, she rubbed a little of the bright green ointment into the boy's eyes, then looked around for the cow. There was no cow as far as she could see, but obeying her orders the girl made the clucking noise she had practiced the night before. There came a sudden *moo* from behind the trees, and a large white cow walked slowly toward them and stood obediently as Cherry milked it. At least she *tried* to milk it, but the instant she placed her hands on the cow's teats, four streams of milk flowed of their own accord and filled the bucket within seconds. She then filled the boy's bowl, and he drank his milk without so much as a word of thanks. Hardly had he drained it than the cow nodded its head and slowly walked away to be lost to sight among the trees.

Aggie had prepared Cherry's breakfast, and while she ate it, the old woman told her that she must keep to the kitchen and attend to her work–scald the milk, make the butter, and clean all the platters and bowls with water and sand. She was not to go into any other part of the house, and above all, she was not to try to open any locked doors. Cherry kept nodding her head and muttering, "Yes, mum."

And so the first week went by, Aunt Aggie sitting with one eye on her knitting and the other boring through poor Cherry–or at least that was what it felt like. Now and again the old woman would grumble to herself, muttering, "I knew Robin would bring back some fool from Zennor. Better none than 'er!"

But Cherry and her master got on famously, working together in the garden picking the apples and pears, which seemed to grow again as soon as they were taken, and weeding the flower beds which the girl noticed seemed never to fade. Aggie was jealous–that was obvious–and one day, although the girl had done nothing wrong, struck her across the back with a broom handle. As luck would have it, her master came around the corner of the house just as it happened and immediately dragged the old woman away.

"Pack your things, you old hag! You're going back to Nancledra."

After that, Cherry was mistress of the house, and her master was so kind and loving that a whole year passed by like a summer day. Occasionally he left home for as long as a week at a time. When he returned, he would spend much time in what Cherry had come to call the enchanted rooms, rooms she had not yet entered. It was then that she could hear him talking to the unknown, but try as she might she could never understand his words.

One day, when her master was absent, Cherry decided to experiment with the magic ointment. She knew it was magic by the way the little boy's eyes pierced and sparkled in so strange a fashion. That day, when the child was washed, his eyes anointed, and the cow milked, she sent him away to gather some flowers at the other end of the garden. She still had the crystal box in her hand, and no sooner was the child out of sight than she put in her little finger, took out a dab of ointment, and smeared it on one eye.

At first she thought her eye would be burned out of her head, it smarted so much. She ran to the pool beneath the rock, holding her hand over her eyes. In doing so, she accidentally rubbed ointment into her other eye with much the same effect, though as soon as she splashed water into them the smarting eased and then stopped.

It was then, as she was gazing into the water, that she saw at the bottom of the crystal pool not one but dozens of tiny little people playing happily–and there was her master, as small as the others, playing with them. Everything in the garden now looked different. Small people were everywhere, hiding in the flowers, swinging in the trees, and running and leaping over the tufts of grass. Many of the little ladies were finely dressed and decked out in golden jewelry and diamonds. Everywhere Cherry looked, she saw the small people's world, and she could now hear their chatter and understand their language. Fascinated, she followed a group of ladies who were off, so they said, to change their jewels. Cherry saw them arrive at a jet-black stone set at the bottom of the granite wall, and she distinctly heard one of the grand little ladies say:

"Stone, stone, black as night,
Open so we see the light,
Trencrom!"

No sooner had she said this final word than, with an audible click, the

stone slid aside to reveal a cave. It glinted and glimmered and sparkled and shone from the reflection of a thousand jewels of gold and silver and precious stones. Cherry held her breath as one by one the little ladies disappeared inside, to reappear minutes later wearing different jewelry. Some now wore ropes of pearls, while others were busy inserting diamond and ruby earrings. As the last one came out, she turned around so that her face and hair were lit up by the flashing of the jewels still inside. She repeated the words:

> "Stone, stone, black as night,
> Close the store of our delight,
> Trencrom!"

And with a click the stone was back in place, sealing the entrance. In the meantime Cherry was repeating the rhymes to herself, determined to learn them both by heart so that one day, perhaps, she could be decked out in finery as good as any lady from Penzance. Her master never showed himself above the water all day, yet as night fell there he was, back to his human size and greeting Cherry as though nothing whatever had happened. Only when he looked in her eyes did he seem puzzled for a moment, but she smiled and pointed to his table, which was laid for supper, and he said no more.

In the morning her master was off again, dressed as if to follow the hounds, but once again she saw him sporting with the fine little ladies under the water. The one Cherry called "the queen" he seemed especially fond of, and when she saw him actually kiss her, she felt a flush of jealousy and realized she was in love. He was back home again at nightfall, ate his supper in a silence Cherry refused to break, then went off to the secret rooms. A few minutes later Cherry crept after him, coming at last to the door through which he had disappeared. She could hear music and laughter and because of the magic ointment could understand all that was said. Putting her eye to the keyhole Cherry peered into the room. Sure enough, there was her master chasing and cuddling the ladies while the one dressed like a queen sat playing a clavichord and singing a love song. When once again she saw him kiss

his ladylove, Cherry grew mad with jealousy and made her way in tears to bed. The next day her master remained at home to gather fruit, but when he turned to give Cherry his customary morning kiss, she burst into tears and told him to go and kiss the small people like himself, with whom he played under the water and in the secret rooms.

"You've used the ointment!"

His face flamed with anger as Cherry hung her head. Then, though she pleaded with him to let her stay, he told her she must return to her own home. With a click of his fingers he disappeared from view, giving her only two hours to collect and pack her things.

As the clock chimed the hour he was back again, and seeing the girl's sad face, he relented so far as to say that, although old Aggie was to come back for the time being, he might one day meet Cherry on Lady Downs moor when her banishment was ended. Then he gave her a bundle of fine clothes such as the small people wore, but miraculously, they fitted Cherry perfectly.

They set out together and walked for many miles, all the time going uphill through lanes and narrow passages. When at last they came to level ground, the master kissed Cherry lightly on her forehead, told her she was bound to be punished for her curiosity, but he would not make it so severe as never to see her again. If she behaved well he might one day take her back to the beautiful garden. Saying this he disappeared.

The sun was high in the heavens, and there was Cherry, seated on a granite stone, without a living soul within miles of her. Long, long did Cherry sit in sorrow, until at last hunger drove her to make her way slowly home. Her parents had long since thought her dead, and when she first opened the cottage door as dusk was falling, they thought her to be her own ghost.

When at last they believed it was their daughter they had given up for dead, they were overjoyed and crowded around her, setting a bowl of broth and a hot pasty before her. Between mouthfuls she told her story, leaving out only the magical rhyme that could open the little cave where the gold and jewels were hidden. This she kept to herself, for if her master kept his promise and took her back to the beautiful garden, she hoped one day to be decked out in finery just like the other ladies. No one else must know that secret or someone might search and search and discover the black stone. Only when quite alone did she say the word "Trencrom."

For the first few weeks Cherry was obedient to her parents and good in every way, but on moonlit nights she would don her shawl and climb Trewey Hill to Lady Downs. Sometimes she was seen sitting on the granite rock by the milestone that pointed the way to Gurnard's Head and New Mill. She was always back in her parents' cottage before dawn, with her mother waiting anxiously for the click of the latch, though often the whole house was asleep before Cherry returned.

And then, a year to the day of her homecoming, or so they said, there was no click of the latch. She has never been seen from that day to this.

The Witch of Fraddam

Where Lord Pengerswick came from no one knew. He and his beautiful lady, attended by two servants, were seen by the astonished inhabitants of Marazion riding high-spirited Arabian horses along the shores of Mount's Bay. From which direction they had come and where they were going remained a mystery until they were seen to dismount near the ruins of Pengerswick Castle. They appeared to have gold in abundance, for in a marvelously short time (some said in only three days!) the castle that bore his name was completely rebuilt, yet none of the local fisherfolk and tin miners saw as much as a single granite block being moved. All the building was done during the dark hours of the night, and all agreed that it was by the force of his enchantments and by the spell of Lady Pengerswick's wonderful voice, which compelled the spirits of the air to work for them. Just three nights were sufficient to raise the enormous castle, and another to furnish it with most beautiful and costly goods, which seemed to appear at the entrance drawbridge as of their own accord.

Soon it came to be believed that the lord and his lady had come from far-off Japan, for they and their servants spoke some Eastern tongue that no Cornishman could understand. Often at night, especially when storms crashed their waves against the very walls of his castle, Pengerswick could be heard for hours on end calling up the spirits by reading from his books in some unknown tongue. On these occasions his voice would roll through the halls louder than the surging waves that beat against the rocks, the spirits replying like the roar of thunder. Fearful indeed was the strife between the enchanter and the demons; but if evil spirits seemed to be winning the battle, his wife would intervene. Whenever the strife became really serious, her harp would be heard making the sweetest and softest music. At this the spirits always fled, and the inhabitants crouching in their cottages would hear them passing overhead toward Land's End, moaning and sighing like a departing storm.

So the weeks turned into months and the months into years, the influence of Lord Pengerswick bringing good health and prosperity to all the poor fisherfolk and farmers and tin miners throughout West Penwith from Hayle to Land's End. Time and again he had reversed the spells of the Witch of Fraddam, the most powerful weird woman in the entire West Country. She had been thwarted so many times that she resolved to destroy Lord Pengerswick by some magic more potent than anything yet heard of, and if she could destroy his Oriental wife as well so much the better.

Firstly, the witch rode on her furze broom over the moors with her black tomcat to Kynance Cove. By spells and incantations she at last succeeded in raising the devil. To him she pledged her soul in exchange for the aid he promised in overthrowing her hated opponent in Pengerswick Castle. The lord's famous Arabian mare was to be seduced to drink from a tub of poisoned water placed by the roadside, the effect of which would be to render the beast so wild and restive as to throw her master immediately to the ground with great force. As Lord Pengerswick lay there wounded, the witch was to drench him instantly with the contents of her crock, containing the most foul and potent hell broth ever concocted, brewed in the blackest night under the most evil aspect of the stars and composed of ingredients that made even the devil shudder. By these means Lord Pengerswick would be forever in the Witch of Fraddam's power, and she might torment him how she pleased forever and a day.

The devil now felt certain of securing the witch's soul, but he was less certain of securing that of the enchanter. It was said that the sorcery Pengerswick had learned in the East was so potent that even Satan himself feared him. So with a smile and a nod of his head he bade her good bye — for the time being!

No sooner had he disappeared, and the smell of brimstone with him, than the witch started to collect, with the utmost care, all the awesome things needed to brew the deadly drink. In the darkest night, in the midst of the wildest storms, amid the flashing of lightning and the bellowing of thunder, she was seen riding her furze broom, on which sat her black tomcat, across the moors and cliffs and mountains in search of her poisons.

At length all was complete, the horse drink was boiled and the hell broth was brewed. It was now March, the time of the equinox. The night was deadly dark and the King of the Storms was abroad. The time was ripe!

The Witch of Fraddam chose her spot carefully, knowing for sure that Lord Pengerswick must pass that way to get back to his castle as she had seen him herself, in her magic mirror, leaving Zennor to cross the moors less than an hour ago. She planted her tub of drink for his horse at the side of the track, while she herself sat crooning in the shadows before her deadly crock of broth.

Fifteen minutes went by; then suddenly the witch heard amid the hurrying winds the heavy tramp of the enchanter's horse. Soon she perceived the outline of man and mare sharply defined against the line of lurid light that stretched its lightning flashes across the western horizon. On, on came horse and rider, the witch hardly able to contain herself between her joy at their imminent overthrow and her fears that his countermagic might ruin her carefully laid plot.

As they neared the tub of drink, the horse snorted loudly and her eyes seemed to flash fire as they looked at the black bowl of poisoned liquid. Instantly Pengerswick bent over the horse's neck and whispered some words into the mare's ear. With incredible speed she turned around, and, lashing out with her hooves, with one mighty kick she scattered all to the wild winds! The tub flew through the air at the terrific blow, crashing into the pot of hell brew, which it overturned, striking a heavy blow against the spindly legs of the Witch of Fraddam, who screamed in pain. She fell alongside the tub, which was changing its form into the shape of a coffin, and her terror was extreme. She, who had thought to unhorse the enchanter and capture him forever, now found herself not only captured, but in a death's-head coffin at the mercy of her enemy.

For a moment all the winds fell silent as Lord Pengerswick raised his voice and gave utterance to some wild words in an unknown tongue, at which even his terrible mare trembled. A whirlwind arose, with the devil himself in the midst of it. Pengerswick snatched up the coffin in which lay the terrified witch, hurled it high into the air, the crock of hell brew following.

"She is settled till the day of doom!" shouted Pengerswick, then spurred his horse and galloped back to his castle.

The Witch of Fraddam still floats high above the cliffs of Cornwall, over the seas and around the coast, still in her coffin and followed by the crock, which looks like a punt in attendance on a larger jolly boat. She still stirs up mischief, churning the sea with her ladle and broom till the waves swell into mountains, heaving foam from their crests and sending up so much spray that these wild wanderers of the winds can scarcely be seen through the mist. Woe to the poor mariner who catches a glimpse of the witch.

Lord Pengerswick alone has power over her. He has but to stand on the tower of his castle and blow three blasts on his silver trumpet to summon her to the shore. With one word he compels her to peace, the winds die down, the waves decrease in size, and all is calm again. Then the Cornish fishermen can set out to sea once more, listening, as they pass the castle, to the sound of Lady Pengerswick's harp and the sweet singing voice that accompanies it.